STAR THISTLE

TERSE VERSE
BY
JIM GRONVOLD

STAR THISTLE

TERSE VERSE

BY
JIM GRONVOLD

Oak Ink Press
2017

Copyright © 2017 Jim Gronvold
Revised Edition
All rights reserved

ISBN-10: 0-9987189-0-4
ISBN-13: 978-0-9987189-0-3

Typesetting: Wordsworth, San Geronimo, CA
Cover photo: Jim Gronvold

To order additional copies of *Star Thistle*
or to contact the author, write:

Oak Ink Press
oakinkpress@icloud.com

To my dear Ann

Contents

Aneurism	1
Countdown	2
Here	3
Calm	4
Woven	5
Ribbon Chert	6
Rock Threads	7
Plows	8
Adrift	9
Wild Places	10
Sprawl	11
Old California	12
Land	13
Caves	14
Slow Learners	15
Skull	16
Curiosity	17
Doubt	18
Uncertainty	19
Thin Air	20

Custom	21
Rumors	22
Planet	23
Diversity	24
Dogma	25
Rivalry	26
Threat	27
Germany 1932	28
Towers	29
Maybe	30
Chain	31
Care	32
Control	33
Guidance	34
Written	35
Passage	36
Harps snd Wings	37
Wise	38
Essence	39
Attention	40
Echoes	41
Fading	42
Try	43

Reward	44
Hours	45
Busy	46
Risen Dust	47
Seasons	48
Dipsea Trail	49
Quiet Pond	50
Meadow Surf	51
Douglas Fir	52
Star Thistle	53
Red-Tailed Hawk	54
Botanical Garden	55
Tern	56
Starlings	57
Car Wings	58
Diner	59
Simple Pleasures	60
Sweet Mundane	61
Emily D.	62
Dylan Thomas' Shed	63
Just One	64
Tavern	65

Leaving	66
Lessons	67
Shoes	68
In Constable's Vale	69
Park Swing	70
Brief	71
Sorrow	72
Stone	73
Trust	74
Shadows	75
Shade	76
Solar Impulse	77
A Summer Evening	78
Inflight Sunset	79
Intent	80

Aneurism

Without warning I fell
gasping for breath

in deep stabbing pain
as I filled with blood—

black lava coursing
through my core—

from a broken vein
that sprang the flood

dragging me out
of consciousness

kicking and screaming
in mortal distress

afraid to let go
too weak to care

struggling to catch
a mouthful of air

fighting the pull
of swirling darkness.

Jim Gronvold

Countdown

Water joins cloud.
Breath becomes breeze.

Hours compute
by minute degrees.

Summer bleeds fall.
Snowflakes breed spring.

We— rise— decline
and return to it all

while every other drifting thing
floating on the star-capped sea

pulls us along somehow
as time counts down to now.

Here

Life itself
is paradise
and whatever
hell that happens.

It makes no claim
on eternity
and needs no name
for divinity

but demands respect
for the powerful truth—
the natural laws
of cause and effect.

Calm

Looking to nature
for peace of mind

it helps to be still
in order to find

the breath we borrow
and will leave behind.

Woven

Billions of evolutions
connected by actions
of cause and effect

that wove and weave
what needs select

as we conceive
threads of our own

and sow seeds
shed from stars

among the wonders
where we were sown.

Ribbon Chert

Rock pages stacked
on their broken spines

are piled along
the coastal shelf.

Each layered leaf
took years to scribble

its record of Earth
rewriting itself

in riddles that crumble
to pebble and sand

on ripples of rock
that jot the headland.

Rock Threads

High folds of ocean
explode over rock

and fall into patterns
of foam-white lace.

Fine cascades
of streaming threads

that weave their way
back out to sea

or rise into mist
and clouds that trace

the rolling edge
of drifting space.

Jim Gronvold

Plows

Spawn of it all
in the great swirling.

Fish evolving
out of the storm.

Scales that swam into
feather and wing

and the long-tailed seed
of the human form

dreaming itself
out of dust to sing

the rippling echo
of everything

on this rolling sphere
that we're wearing down

with too many plows
on its thin veneer.

Adrift

Some waves open
windows as they break

and scatter sparkles
on sand in their wake.

Translucent walls
of liquid light

slamming shut
over and over

revealing currents
in constant motion

on the wet skin
of the deep core

where our spinning sphere
churns the molten ocean

that we drift on
from shore to shore.

Jim Gronvold

Wild Places

In those wild places
we would love to live
but would spoil
by building houses

you take a picture,
a leaf, or a stone
to hang on a wall
or set on a shelf

to remember
the beauty
no person
should own,
because it belongs
to our deepest self.

Sprawl

Old forests fall
to the chainsaw—

grassland to farmland—
parkland to mall.

Oceans are poisoned
by tainted tide

with oil, plastic,
and pesticide.

We strangle rivers
to fit our plans

and choke the air
out of the sky

but still believe
we have a right

to dominate
and multiply.

Old California

What colors were
these virgin hills
before explorers
spread their stain

and pious missions
promised paradise
to the people of
natural glory

teaching sin
and purgatory
to the children
of sun and rain?

Land

Some people plunder
the wild places
where deer and we
would wander.

Too many think
they have a right
to exploit
every field in sight

and put their profit
before the need
to let more land
return to seed.

Caves

Now we retreat
to cushioned caves
and burn illusions
of flickering light

or draw our visions
with digital strokes
on scrolling walls
in micro-byte—

warm in the thralls
of our distractions—
while sunlight dances
over our graves.

Slow Learners

Grounded in nature
by our long journey
out of elements
that had to collide

before cells could divide
into lives connected
by the time-spun dance
of choice and chance.

We've come pretty far
for slow learners
but still rely
on old stories

that promise bliss
in a stained glass sky
to guide how we live
and hide how we die.

Jim Gronvold

Skull

What better teachers
than the silent stars
or the beating pulse
of waves on shore?

What better speaker
than a hollow skull
to echo the lesson
of nevermore?

Curiosity

We wonder and wander
from answer to answer

beyond the limits
of certainty

and follow our
own curiosity

through every kind
of circumstance

learning the ways
of reality

on this shining sphere
in the vast expanse.

Doubt

Knowing the need
to understand
what it all
is all about,

I also know
the freedom
of not needing
to figure it out,

of feeling enough
uncertainty
to value the
wisdom of doubt.

Uncertainty

We may never
be able to know

the source of the cause
that scattered the stars

and every effect
that led to the next

as ripples stepped
in and out of each other

stirring smoke into
planets and shining seas

and dust into
dreamers of fantasies

who seem to believe
it was all done for them.

Jim Gronvold

Thin Air

Believe in legends
that can't be proved

or take leaps of faith
into thin air—

hoping to land
on a cloud somewhere—

and miss the beauty
within our reach

by trading sunlight
for a fantasy.

Custom

Not the blind faith
of certainty

nor the poor vision
of narrow view.

Neither perspective
convinces me

that I may not know
what is right and true

by putting my trust
in reality

and not letting custom
define what I see.

Jim Gronvold

Rumors

First we believe
there is just one way

and then we distrust
any other.

Our narrow vision
turns shadow to fear.

Habits of mind
find changes to dread.

We fight each other
over rumors we hear

and children bury
the innocent dead.

Planet

Thinking beyond
mythology, religion,
or ideology

how can it be
so hard to agree
that the raw beauty
of wild nature
deserves our
deepest respect.

And how can we
not do more
to protect what's left
of our legacy

before it's buried
under all our crap,
and we turn this planet
into toxic scrap?

Jim Gronvold

Diversity

The sea
in the cloud
in the rain.

The field
in the stalk
in the grain.

The they
in the you
in the me,

all sing
the truth
of diversity.

Dogma

Dogmas that deny
the facts of death

may tell stories
we'd like to believe.

Those ancient visions
of eternal breath

may comfort us
when we grieve

but can also lead
the sad or naive

to blindly follow
devout extremes

and fall prey to
oppressive regimes.

Jim Gronvold

Rivalry

While competition
may bring out our best
it can just as well
bring out our beast.

Consider the people
who need to prove
that they're better
than all the rest.

And then connect
greed to poverty
and the savage hell
of armed conquest.

Threat

Dangerous extremes
stuck on points of view
deny common ground

and shout opinions
as if repetition
could prove them true.

Their promises
treat blind faith
as if it were a virtue

but the knives come out
when questioned about
the truth of their
grand little schemes.

Jim Gronvold

Germany 1932

Voters who fell for
the lies of a bully

empowered a reign
of tyranny

that rose out of
hatred and poverty

and led to the horror
of millions of dead

for delusions of
glorious destiny.

Towers

The forces of evil
are all too human.
They feed on our fear
and enshrine their greed.

They lie to the poor
from golden towers;
dine on fine china
while nations bleed

and lead the world
toward self-destruction
from behind the mask
of their selfish creed.

Maybe

If we think
it through
to the consequences

with the aid
of whatever
common sense is

we might
treat each other
with the respect

that we think
we have
a right to expect.

Chain

When I recognize
a feeling I know
in someone else's
laughter or pain,

or the meaning of
a revealing look
that no one person
could contain,

I touch a thread
of something stronger
than fables or creeds
could ever explain

and begin to grasp
a bit of a link
in an ever
evolving chain.

Jim Gronvold

Care

In the spirit
of true compassion
actions embody
our best intentions.

Not oratory,
or civic pretensions.
Not good excuses,
or large donations.

But simple care
and consideration
for anyone
not as lucky as you.

Star Thistle

Control

On the shadow side of this quiet fjord
a windmill chops at the evening sky
as if it were winding down the sun.

An empty rowboat sways nearby
seeming to guide the turning tide
from the end of its rusty chain.

And a vain rooster weather vane
follows the shifting airflow
pointing the way as if to direct
where the wind is meant to go.

Jim Gronvold

Guidance

Why ask for guidance
when it's all around
in every process
from the stars to the ground?

Why look forward
to what's already here
as if better days
were bound to appear?

And why look backwards
at what isn't there
or ask the sky
as if it could care?

Written

Opinions interpret
what's written in stone.

Those old translations
of superstitions

and hallowed myths
of long dead shadows

that carry the weight
of the dust they intone

and the wars they compose
with the words they hone.

Jim Gronvold

Passage

Waiting for angels
that do not appear

we may treat this life
like a passageway

to some better place
or a finer day.

And how does that
help us embrace

what little time
we have right here?

Harps and Wings

When purveyors
of pious authority
painted heaven on clouds
and hell on flames

they tried to sway
the suffering masses
with fearful warnings
and fanciful claims

promising prizes
of harps and wings
in glorious realms
of eternal rapture.

But for anyone
who disagreed,
the reward was
endless torture.

Wise

Nothing I see
convinces me
that I can live
beyond my breath.

Watching the way
all things decay
makes me think
it would be wise

not to count
on a better deal
anytime after
my sad demise.

Essence

It may not be
a spark we inherit
or a pale shadow
of who we were.

It may not look like
a Renaissance angel
or sound like
a phantom whisper.

It might just be
an energy
that body and brain
produce together.

A synergy
of flesh and fancy
that we recognize
in each other.

Jim Gronvold

Attention

Would believing
in life after death
make me more aware
of each sweet breath?

Would I enjoy
this cup of tea
any more than
I already do?

Would believing
in immortality
make any moment
more important to me?

Would I pay more
attention to time,
without a sense
of finality?

Echoes

Threads of connection
are everywhere:

in the soil that feeds us
and the air we borrow,

in the music we hear
and the stories we share,

in crowded laughter
or lonesome sorrow.

All our sensations
have echoes somewhere—

connections between
the here and there—

subtle reflections
of now on tomorrow.

Jim Gronvold

Fading

All things pass
and in their passing
the fact of fading
is reality—

a truth we deny
when we believe
inventions of
immortality.

Try

If I chose to rely
on providence
and tried to deny
impermanence,

I might now believe
I would never die,
but every death
would prove it a lie.

So why not accept
the evidence—
employ a bit
of commonsense—

and choose to enjoy
this experience,
for as long as
I'm able to try?

Reward

We dream beyond
the day-to-day

and lose the hours
that we've ignored.

But treat this life
as all you have

and breath becomes
its own reward.

Hours

Wearing ruts between
dawn and gone

the circles we churn
running around

whirl into eddies
while daylight reels

spinning our wheels
as hours turn

and twist in the wind
or twirl on the ground

while winter approaches
or spring is unwound.

Jim Gronvold

Busy

When there's always
somewhere to go,
something to do,
or someone to see

when do we stop
long enough to know
how it really feels
just to simply be?

Risen Dust

A strolling fog
tips its brim
and sky drips
down a rocky rim
quiet as cloud
gliding past moon
or sunlight sliding
over a log.

No need to kneel
at carved altars
or sing in hallowed halls
to praise the mist
that raises dust
with resurrecting rain
or the falling stars
that fill the spray
of sacred waterfalls.

Seasons

Seasons attended
through open doors

are secular spaces
for simple rites

of reverence
for natural beauty

that needs no temple
nor grand cathedral—

no ceremony
or acolytes—

to hear the word
the wind recites.

Dipsea Trail

Down the ocean end
of the ridge top trail

through the scent
of sunburned chaparral

between fog pine
and sparkling brine

to the green shade
of the spindly forest

where sunlight flutters
through the shingled veil

I close my eyes
and just inhale

the brief heaven
of a laurel leaf.

Jim Gronvold

Quiet Pond

This pond can be
postcard still

until the bluegill
poke ripples at flies

or a cool breeze
skips leaf shadows

over drifting reflections
of October skies.

Meadow Surf

Spring breezes spill
down sky swept hills

in wave patterns
of choppy grasses.

The swirling flow
of ruffled green

bubbling with poppy
and purple lupine

bobbing on currents
of rolling meadow

below the billowing
whitecaps on blue

that drift the valleys
their shadows renew.

Jim Gronvold

Douglas Fir

A ruin wall
of pressed root—

the webbed foot
of a fallen tree—

probably a Douglas Fir,
toes up, on the forest floor.

Could be the victim
of a violent storm

left to decay
in leafy shadows

where it now is host
to seed and spore

on this shallow crust
of crowded compost

where generations
of fir fell before.

Star Thistle

On fire road trails
in the hills we hike,
Yellow Star Thistle
is standing sentry
with morningstar spikes
of thorny bristle—

an innocent armor
that shares a shape
our ancestors
used as weapons.

That weedy gentry
of dusty domain
guards its patch
of stolen turf
from marauding birds
and grazing herds,
jauntily flaunting
a flaxen-plumed crown,
as it holds its ground
against the wild grasses

and the sharp blades
of the well clipped town,
down by the freeway
forever attacking.

Jim Gronvold

Red-Tailed Hawk

I saw a Red-Tail
with wings full of light

crossing its path
on a bright blue sky.

A translucent being
so full of grace

that it suddenly dropped
an unwinding scroll

of cloud-white
angelic ribbon

to bless the bone-dry
fields below

with a miracle
of summer snow.

Star Thistle

Botanical Garden

Wandering through the Botanical Garden
on a fine afternoon in Copenhagen,

I noticed a patch of odd little flowers
and wondered if they had a name I would know.

So I climbed the path to a gatekeeper's hut
where an ancient fellow in uniform

slowly appeared with a long white beard
and eyes as blue as the sky behind him

which made his face look like a mask
held against the heavens of summer.

When I asked in a whisper of broken Danish
if there was a list of plant names in English

he answered in a voice of gravel and grit
"De er alle de somme lort": ("It's all the same shit.").

Jim Gronvold

Tern

From a sharp glide
over clear water

a bright Tern spins
toward a flash of fin

on honed feathers,
rudder and wing

that swing its beak
into arrow aim

and the ocean
never feels the sting.

Starlings

Evening Starlings
slide past my windshield

descending like rain
across rush hour traffic

in a furious cloud
sliding into a curve

to swerve under
this old truss bridge

in their race to roost
with the screeching crowd

that I hear beneath
this gridlocked span

where I sit—crawling
my own way home.

Jim Gronvold

Car Wings

Those arms stretching out
of the windows ahead

might have been mine
a few years ago.

Fingers spread
to catch the air

or flattened to slice
its rushing flow—

twisting like flaps
on airplane wings—

Scratching the sky
of highway summer

the way we did
when we flew on swings.

Diner

Blue plate special
in a vinyl booth

or a short stack
on a chrome stool.

Bacon and eggs,
sunny-side up,

and hot java
in a bottomless cup.

Before I get back
on that long road,

think I'll have a slice
of pie a la mode.

Simple Pleasures

Aroma of coffee.
Flavor of tea.

Sweet-sour stir-fry
or pumpkin pie.

Why do we wish
for bliss in the sky

while innocent
pleasures are plenty?

Why not inhale
the scent of trees

or the wild sea
on a soft breeze

and appreciate
some paradise

before it's
too damn late.

Sweet Mundane

With luck you'll wake up
to the sweet mundane

without a worry
or any real pain

and not have to waste
the precious morning

on anything you're
still waiting for

but be able to own
the time you spend

and enjoy what you have
without needing more.

Emily D.

Not by the book—
she wrote off the hook—

and wriggling free
broke the rigid line

to catch the sea
in a puddle of window

before she let
the wild thing go.

Dylan Thomas' Shed

His voice kept the dust
off those windows awhile
in that shed above
the Welsh bay
where he watched
spires of seabirds scud

and the tide slide
over mussel shell mud
on the watery wide
cloud-way of heaven
that he tethered to
the weathered perch,
where words went to fly.

Jim Gronvold

Just One

One for courage.
One to forget.

Two would follow
itself to three.

Four turned into
too many more

and all too often
a time to regret

until zero became
a better bet.

Tavern

Our tavern lit up
the back street
where we sparkled
like shattered glass.

Our laughter spun
down a spiral
of tables that turned
on a round

or floated
between chatter

and silences
waiting to pass

until we scattered
into our echoes
and staggered off
to run aground.

Jim Gronvold

Leaving

Some of us wander
as if we knew where,

leaving the places
or people we blame

to find whatever
wasn't back there

but only end up
with more of the same

and may not feel
at home—anywhere.

Lessons

Happy as only
the once lost can be.

Cautious as only
the wounded are wise.

Honest as only
the cheated may try.

We learn our skills
accordingly

and find a better way,
or three,

but miss our chance
if we agonize

over what's over
or yet to be.

Jim Gronvold

Shoes

If my only address
was this pair of shoes

where would I spend
the freezing night?

Would I numb my pain
with cut-rate booze

and crash in a corner
until daylight?

Would I sink so far
I'd give up the fight

if I thought I had
nothing left to lose?

In Constable's Vale

"The Vale of Dedham"
painted in 1828.

Hidden from the mill
and the church tower town

in a mannered shire
of the hallowed crown

a Gypsy lady
holding a baby

huddles by a fire
near a tattered tent

between fields, poplars,
river and foxglove

while dark clouds twist
into tears above

the humble mother
shields her fierce love.

Jim Gronvold

Park Swing

Memory aching
at the gentle sight
of a mother and child
on a swing.

Suspended and still
in the arcing light
between back and forth—
birth and mourning.

Happiness
in the balance
between innocence
and night.

Brief

Seeing how
we rise and fall
through any
average lifespan

we find our time
is all too brief
and enjoy it
while we can

or try to trust
an old belief
that promises
timeless bliss

and miss the forest
in a leaf
or the sunlight
in a kiss.

Jim Gronvold

Sorrow

The fact of death,
though full of sorrow,
may inspire
a fresh desire

to live as well
as life is brief

and laugh again,
though deep in grief.

Stone

Looking for any connection
to feelings that once felt like home,

for a thread of the old certainty
that made the world seem whole,

I stumbled over a dusty stone
that had an odd little hole

and wondering how it came to be,
it suddenly occurred to me

that even something that solid
had endured changes of its own.

Trust

A simple trust
in returning sun

can calm the dread
of descending night

remembering that
as time is spun

darkness is also
followed by light.

Shadows

Among the standing dead
a woodpecker beats his drum.

Vultures spread their dark capes
over the bones of branches.

Shadows drag crawling shapes
over whispering ferns.

An owl screams overhead
and the wind begins to hum.

Autumn sends a shiver
of darker days to come.

Then a chipmunk chuckles
somewhere near
and the phantoms disappear.

Shade

Squinting at
sunlight squeaking
through branches

pinpoint prisms
halo sharp edges
of luminous leaves

as sinking sun weaves
down the scaled shade
into shadows already
crawling toward night.

Solar Impulse

*The first sun-powered
airplane to circle
the globe, in 2016.*

A silver sliver
in the sunset sky,
an aircraft advancing
over the ocean
on a ripple
of harnessed light.

A wind-beaten whisper
drumming the air
humming toward shore
under spreading night

on its way around
the spinning world
as the human inside
those solar cell feathers,
pushes the limits
of dream-powered flight.

Jim Gronvold

A Summer Evening

Flaming clouds stretch overhead.

Colors that only colors can tell
spread across the evening sky.

Clouds bleeding light as seconds die
in burning splendor or blushing pastel.

A beauty that cannot be painted or said
but can be enjoyed before last light has fled.

Inflight Sunset

Cloud scattered
streaks of sunlight
fall copper on
deep blue water—

broken by shadows
of islands—
as we climb above
the shrinking coast
on the steep thin air
of October.

Sunset burns
the bottoms of clouds
that glow like coals
under sky-soft cobbles

until the sun gives up its ghost
from a spark sinking in dark ocean
while rising as dawn somewhere.

Intent

Let life be my religion
and appreciation my prayer.

May reason and passion guide
however long I taste sweet air.

www.ingramcontent.com/pod-product-compliance
Lightning Source LLC
Chambersburg PA
CBHW070548300426
44113CB00011B/1824